To: _____

From: _____

Date: _____

Copyright © 2023 Susan Windsor

Published by Mad Hatter Communications, LLC.

All rights reserved.

ISBN: 978-1-961515-10-9 (soft cover)

ISBN: 978-1-961515-11-6 (hard cover)

Made in United States
Orlando, FL
05 March 2024